The Action Plan

The Action Plan

How to Implement the Law of Attraction into Your Life in Under an Hour

By Natasha Grano

Printed in the United States of America

First Printing, 2020

ISBN-13: 978-1-949003-54-3 print edition
ISBN-13: 978-1-949003-55-0 ebook edition

Waterside Productions
2055 Oxford Ave
Cardiff, CA 92007
www.waterside.com

Prologue

From the bottom of my heart I want to thank the following friends for giving me the opportunity to write this.. Without you it would never have been possible. Elijah Rowen, for guiding me through every word of this book. Rebecca Riofrio for opening the doors to make this even possible. Mirela Sula for believing in me. Lucas Serby for editing so patiently. Waterside Publishing for giving me this incredible opportunity. For all those who have helped me, I know the universe will give you unlimited opportunities in return. I wish for everyone who reads this that your light too will shine so bright it will light up the whole universe and together we can make the world a better place.

I love you

Natasha x

Introduction

Once you're done reading this book, the life you've been dreaming of will immediately begin. You will be equipped with the tools for success, wealth, perfect health, happiness, love - anything you can think of. Once you begin reading this book, you will be in the right mindset to start achieving. I want to help cure you of any possible illness, lack of purpose, depression, self sabotage - anything that negatively affects you - in the same way I cured myself first. These are words I wish somebody had given me before I made all the mistakes I made, although having made those mistakes, I can help prevent you from making them and give you a shortcut to... your perfect life.

Chapters

Ask yourself:

Are you proactive or are you happy to let the days simply pass you by?

Do you have courage or are you content enough to curl up in a ball and hide away from the world?

Do you have faith in the fact that you've beaten the odds by merely being here, and know that you can do it again?

Do you understand that you have something authentic to offer the world?

Are you riding the wave of excitement or are you allowing negativity to suck you in?

You can make whatever you will of the universe, are you going to just exist in it or actually make your mark on it?

Do you have gratitude for the advantages you've been given over others on this planet?

Are you tolerant of difference and appreciate that you don't have to control others?

Are you truly putting love into the world and elevating those around you in a solely positive way?

Proactive over Passive

Often in life, you will come upon a path that diverts in two different directions. These two different paths are often not obvious, because one of the routes is quite simply staying where you are and not treading any new ground at all. The other route is new unexplored territory (whatever that might be). It could be anything from learning a new instrument, to making that phone call that you're too intimidated to make, to taking the first step towards a whole new career path. These two paths are what I call the Proactive and the Passive paths.

I, for one, can not think of any one time in my life where the passive route was the way to go, and as mad as it sounds, saying "I wish I hadn't done that" is not nearly as bad a phrase as "I wish I had…".

"Comfort is the enemy of growth" - Unknown

I know a man, let's call him Chazz, who has a skillset that he was either born with or that he developed along the road, but this particular skill-set I believe would have him equal to frontmen of the likes of Mick Jagger and Bono. And, funnily enough, would have him measure up to the comedy skills of Ricky Gervais or Lenny Henry. Now this guy Chazz is in his mid-twenties and still lives with his mother and has to hit her up for twenty bucks every time he even wants to go out for a couple of drinks with his mates. A sad situation altogether; especially for a man with such an outstanding skillset. The problem with this situation is that he has quite simply become far too comfortable. Be weary of being too comfortable in any area of your life. You will lose that want and that need to grow. You will end up becoming stale and not taking from life what you could, or worse: not actually finding any purpose in life at all.

"Find comfort in the discomfort." - *Unknown*

If you're in a warm bed in a cold room and your alarm rings at 6 am because it's time to go to the gym, it's going to be pretty damn difficult to get up and go, as you're far too comfortable laying right where you are. You need to look forward to getting out of bed. Give yourself a good reason that excites you every day, or you're not you're not going to be living the life you should be. I'm going to give you something right now that I want you to try during your next shower/bath and I guarantee you it's going to benefit you in many ways, physically as well as mentally.

Exercise:

After you've had your next warm shower/bath, you're going to turn the temperature down to the coldest it can be and then you're going to stay there in that freezing water for as long as you can take. Try it, even if you can only do it for 10 seconds to start with, and build up each day up to a few minutes if you can. Now, I can guarantee you that's going to take you out of your comfort zone immediately. It's also going to tremendously benefit you, as crazy as that might sound to some, and I'm going to give you a few reasons why right now, and we're going to dive into much more specific and scientific detail at the end of the book. But for now, just know: this does a monumental amount for your body, and one of the things it does for your mind is it actually promotes emotional resilience, which will ward off stress and depression and give you a much greater defence against those things.

As brilliant as this technique is, and as much as it has genuinely helped me, the reason I'm going to encourage you to do this as soon as possible is that it is a blatant step in the right direction, and it's a step you can take immediately. Making a change in any way can be difficult, but know that the first step is often the most difficult, and so, I'd like you to see this first step in this particular area as symbolic, and as a step in the right direction, in so many different areas.

Remember this: in life you have got to do what you don't want to do to be able to do what you want to do.

You have got to dig that ditch even though you don't want to do it, you've got to make that call even though your ego doesn't want you to, you've got to do that workout even though it's so much easier not to. If you want to get ahead in life, start enjoying the things you don't want to do with that in mind. You are laying tracks for your future.

You are going to prove to yourself today that you are good enough, and you owe it to yourself to step up and be the best version of yourself that you can be. You never know where these things might lead you, but I can tell you where not doing them will lead you: nowhere.

Thoughts will influence the way you are feeling everyday. However, possessions and goals are not achieved through thought alone. They are achieved through proactiveness, courage, wisdom and faith in yourself. There are a lot of wealthy individuals out there, and it sounds cliche to say that money doesn't equal happiness, but it's true. That being said, if you possess the tools to achieve whatever you want to achieve and utilise those tools, then wealth is a by-product that will undoubtedly be bestowed upon you. Remember though, if you seek only materialistic possessions, and emit malice into the world in order to get them, you will ultimately get that same energy back. Whatever actions you take, do so with kindness, love and gratitude, and with all the wonderful things you've achieved, you will feel that same wonder right back. You will be able to enjoy your achievements to the fullest and will lift up so many others to do the same thing along the road. Now, let's delve into the things that will get you into that powerful zone of achievement right now. As you are already reading this I know you are well capable of stepping into that zone, so enjoy the ride…

Courage over Anxiety

Did you know that the part of the brain that runs amuck when you're stricken with anxiety is the very same part of the brain that does that very same thing for a warthog when he sees a ravenous lion sprinting at him? I think you should find some comfort in that, however heavy anxiety may often times seem, at least there isn't a ravenous lion about to tear you to pieces (well hopefully there isn't anyway).

I'm going to tell you about how different people's minds work, and even if your friend seems like they're having an easier time than you in what might seem like a similar situation to the outside eye, you are not alone in this. Even if it may seem irrational to others, it isn't. Because everyone's minds work completely differently, and once people get more of an understanding of that we can all push each other in the right direction.

Now some people may seem mentally bulletproof, like someone I know very well, a young actor called Elijah Rowen. The man doesn't seem to have an ounce of anxiety at times, when I, for one, would absolutely be bricking it with nerves. I've seen him get up in front of panels of producers and act out scenes that he barely knows the words to and he does it with such conviction that it doesn't even matter. I've also seen him snowboard down a black run (the steepest slope there is) when he's never even been on a snowboard before in his life and survive it, while laughing the whole way down. Now, although these things may make the rest of us very scared, nervous or anxious, the man mustn't feel things that most others do. Do these seemingly courageous acts showcase courage? Not exactly. Hear me out...

Three years ago I was in a very dark place. I had just given birth to my beautiful son which was the best day of my life, and then suddenly I was thrown into being bed bound by an autoimmune disease that attacked me like a grenade out of nowhere. I had to move back in with my parents, and I couldn't even bring myself to leave the house. This wasn't actually because of the illness itself, but because of the immense anxiety it had caused me to have. I would cry every day, fearful that I had lost who I was forever, and imagining that I would be in that state of panic until my final days. I will never forget the day I decided that enough was enough. I would not let my body control me, so I told my body to sit down for a few minutes and listen to me. I told my body it did not control me and that it would now have to listen to my orders and I would in turn nurture it and love it. I gave myself special exercises, which I have revealed for you at the back of this book, and I would do these day after day with the mindset of "I AM ALREADY IN PERFECT HEALTH" and I wouldn't take anything less for an answer. I'm going to go into more detail about these magical exercises later on, but what i'm really getting at here is the fact that I stepped up and had the courage to step out of that comfort zone and do everything in my power to make that change. Now, the Elijah character doesn't need to have that courage to step up, as he doesn't really feel a sense of fear like me or maybe you. It doesn't matter, you don't have to be hard on yourself for being scared or anxious. There is nothing cowardly about having those feelings, so never be hard on yourself for feeling them again.

"I learnt that courage was not the absence of fear but the triumph over it. The brave is not he who does not feel afraid, but he who conquers that fear" - Nelson Mandela

It is important to note that it's the taking of actions that is going to help you overcome this, not just "thinking" about getting over them. Take that step, do what needs to be done. Our thoughts have incredible power when thought with a strong emotional feeling behind them, but make sure that these thoughts are followed up with action or otherwise you're not thinking them with real commitment. Courage can be found within yourself, it is a bit like energy: it is all around us and will never cease to exist. Everyone's going to encounter it, it's whether or not you decide to harness it. And although anxiety is a bunch of thoughts that we cannot control, harnessing that courage that will ultimately triumph over anxiety, is a choice.

"Can a man still be brave if he's afraid? That is the only time a man can be brave, his father told him." - George R.R.Martin, Author of Game Of Thrones.

We have around 40 thoughts a minute, most of which we do not even remember. When we focus on a specific thought, it can spiral out of control very fast. When you start spiralling downwards with negative thoughts about a situation that gives you anxiety, this is honestly only to your own detriment. And the thing to do here is to firstly RECOGNISE that you are spiralling downwards and letting your thoughts run away without you, and then, take the reins back. REPLACE those negative thoughts with all the positive things that could, just as likely (if not more than likely), happen and soon you will have catapulted your way back up to a safe place again. Needless to say, when you've got 40 thoughts a minute, there's a great opportunity there to focus on the positive ones as well. There is a lot of good in this world too. And when we start focusing on that, that is when we conquer our fears. We can't change the world with a thought but we can absolutely change the way we view it.

"Don't see fear or anxiety as an unusual or horrible thing, see it as an opportunity to prove something to yourself." - Elijah Rowen

Exercise:

I cannot emphasise enough the benefits of doing daily breathing exercises. Whenever your thoughts are feeling clouded and you have too many irrational and negative things going through your mind, just breathe that negative energy out. The exercise below is so easy, and you can do it almost anywhere. I encourage you to try this one now and continue doing it daily for forever more:

The Wim Hof breathing exercise:

"While sitting in a comfortable place, take 30 quick, deep breaths, inhaling through your nose and exhaling through your mouth. Then, take a deep breath and exhale; hold until you need to breathe in. Inhale again, as deep as you can, and hold it for 10 seconds. Repeat as many times as you like." - Discover Magazine

Certainty over Insecurity

You might find in everyday life that you're doing a lot of things that wouldn't quite qualify as nice or sweet, despite the fact that you're actually a good person. These actions, however big or small they might be, seem to get the better of you. Other people are making you feel bad about yourself for whatever reason: maybe they're taller than you, maybe they're better at a certain skill than you or maybe it's something as ridiculous and irrelevant as that they have bigger breasts than you. Understand where these nasty comments that you're making towards these people are coming from. Try and find genuine happiness in the fact that this person is better than you at something, because if you had the best of everything in every aspect you would find that you wouldn't have any want for other people in this world, and you would find that everything would get boring very quickly. I've got a theory that everyone is born equal, and even though it may seem as though some have more talents than others and some are more physically attractive than others, believe me, the truly successful in any respect and the truly desirable in any sense of the word are the ones with the right mindset who take the right actions. As cliche as it sounds, be the best version of yourself, and be happy for others who are striving to do the same. You are well and truly only competing with yourself; and rather than battling yourself by thinking that others outshine you, understand that you do not have to have that battle. If you make peace with yourself, you've already won a war that 99% of people will never finish for as long as they live.

"Do not allow negative thoughts to enter your mind, for they are the weeds that strangle confidence" - Bruce Lee

People may have belittled you throughout your life, claiming you have certain negative traits. There's no need to get into the invalidating terminology that I'm sure has been thrown at you by at least one person in your life. Rather just remember this: whatever labels you've been given, whether they're truthful or not (because there's always going to be people in your life who will try to put you down, whether the reasons are valid or not) they are not permanent labels. Recognise these negative labels that you may be carrying with you, and recognise that you can shed them even more easily than you acquired them. Right now, think what labels you've let stay attached to you? They may have come from relatives, colleagues, friends or enemies. We are what we want to be, and do not have to allow other people's words to shape us if they have no positive place in our lives. Go to the root of the problem and don't give it any more power.

'No one can make you feel inferior without your consent' - Eleanor Roosevelt

Imagine if we could apply this same level of certainty to other areas in life, because believe me, it can have that same profound effect. Now, I understand that when someone asks you "Why are you so insecure?" or tells you to "Be more confident" it's as good as useless. Now the old phrase "Fake it til you make it" will probably get you further than not even trying to be more confident and certain in your actions at all. However, the way to make a really powerful and genuine change is to go to the root of the problem. You've got a power inside you just as great as the power inside of anyone else, and I am telling you this with absolute certainty. Do not give this power away. I'm going to give you an example of giving it away that quite a few women are guilty of. If you are insecure about the way men act around you, for instance, it is because you may seek their approval, crave their attention or yearn for something along those lines. Now, by doing this you are taking some of your power and giving it to them. You are giving them power over you. Anything you are feeling insecure about, or any area you are trying to control that you don't really have control over, you are giving power to when there is absolutely no real reason to.

A plant harnesses the sun's rays to produce energy, strength, and life. It doesn't give the power it has harnessed away or it would wither and die. That's not to say you shouldn't help others, you should always use your power to help others and do so with absolute certainty. But don't give that power to them, and don't want to take their power from them either, because that would mean that one of you has power over the other. Craving power over other people is a corrupt desire and is actually a blatant sign of insecurity. Use your power to help others, and I assure you that the law of reciprocation will ensure that it will be reciprocated. Elevate others around you, don't feel inferior to anyone. We are all born with equal power, but it's how we choose to ignite that power that matters. Ignite it with certainty, there is no room for insecurity; and utilise your maximum power which you were born with, which everyone has, and which by all rights you deserve.

'If you don't give your power away to anyone, that's when you can harness your superpower.' - Elijah Rowen

Exercise:

Write a list of positive affirmations that begin with "I AM..." followed by a positive word that describes who you are and who you want to be someday. Learn these by heart, and every morning, stand in your power with your feet firmly on the ground (this is called grounding, which is an exercise that we're going to delve deeper into later on) and smile as you read these aloud, as the act of smiling alone releases endorphins and will put you in a more positive mindset. Thoughts are far more powerful when they have a powerful feeling and emotion behind them. Once you begin to say these affirmations with absolute certainty, that's when they become fact.

Authenticity over Imitation

"There's never any point in trying to be someone else, because the world already has one of them. There's no point in offering the world another one. The only truly unique thing you can offer the world, that it's never seen before, is you." - Elijah Rowen.

Once you are truly authentic to yourself, you will have a much greater clarity of the world. You will be able to emote in a much more honest manner, and express yourself freely. There is so much freedom in being authentic, as you no longer feel the need to appease someone else. There's no longer any pressure to get it right or wrong, because there is no right or wrong. If you're true to yourself you can't go wrong. Take a look at the people around you, how many are dressed unusually similar? These people are following what other people do, as a means to cover up insecurity. It's more than fine to not care about your dress sense, but make sure you are dressing a certain way for the right reasons and not because you want to try and fit in. There's no glory in fitting in and following trends, only in setting them.

"Be yourself; everyone else is already taken." - Oscar Wilde

Remember this; when feeling insecure with any of your unique quirks, the more of an individual you are, the more you have to offer to the world that it hasn't seen before. Embrace this. Be happy that you are not like that popstar or movie star you always wanted to be growing up,because if you were, you would actually just be a lesser version of them, living in their shadow. But as you're not, you can contribute something to the world that it hasn't seen before. Stand up for what you believe in: anything you feel self-conscious about that is truly you, own it. Stand up for it. Because there is actually nothing more likeable than a person that owns who they are. The smallest things, for instance, such as a foreign kid showing up to school with a lunchbox completely different to any of the other kids. If he attempts to hide his lunch and becomes insecure about the look, smell or taste of it, he makes himself easy prey. However, if he owns it, jokes about it and even brags that he gets to eat something completely unique with great confidence, then he can completely turn the tables; becoming a trend setter, a leader - an authentic person.

Don't worry about being as good as someone else is at something, worry about being the best version you can be. No one can compete with that. The enjoyment you will receive from no longer being insecure about who you are is an incredible feeling. Once you are confident in who you are you can set trends, and the weight off your shoulders of not having to follow feels amazing. A man I know, let's call him Mac, has stopped caring about what others think of him. He was once very attractive, a fairly ordinary guy who carried that weight on his shoulders, trying to fit in. He was from what most of us would see as an ordinary background, and had all of the ordinary hang ups, insecurities and problems with himself that most people do. He now often dresses in garments ranging from womens boots, to purple top hats to open jackets with no shirt on. And he doesn't apologise for it. It's who he is. It's what he feels like doing and it's not hurting anyone else. He does it with great confidence, that it's the only way to be, and the result is a very magnetic individual. And an individual who no longer has to worry about fitting in, being insecure about his clothing, or having to appease anyone else. You only have one life. Enjoy it, enjoy being who you are, let go of hang ups others have stuck on you, enjoy leading fearlessly - it's an amazing feeling. And it is a feeling of great freedom. This isn't a dress rehearsal - this is the real show, baby. Give it everything you have, give it your all.

Here are some questions that actually matter, answer them truthfully:

What is your objective in life (what do you want over anything)?
What obstacles might you encounter along the road of achieving this objective?
What are you willing to do to surpass those obstacles?

Take your time. Once you have answered the questions you will understand more about who you are - your character.

Faith over Pessimism

Focusing on positive things you want to happen is a far better place to be in than dwelling on negative scenarios that you cannot control. There are both rational and irrational fears. If you want to dwell on them, there is no end to things to be pessimistic or fearful of, and even me giving those too much thought would result in me being pessimistic to some degree. I'm going to give you an example of some irrational pessimism based on fear. There are many people that, when they get on a plane, for some irrational reason become incredibly fearful that, for some reason, the plane is going to crash, and that it could be the end for them (by the way I was one of those people once). Let me just put this into perspective people: you are nearly 100 times more likely to die in a car crash than a plane crash. Now, a lot of people have probably missed out on a lot of opportunities, or given themselves horrendous anxiety for a few hours over something that there is no reason to focus on. So what I am saying is this: even though nothing is going to happen either way, you have just let nothing ruin those few hours. Now imagine if you had faith that nothing can harm you and that nothing was going to go wrong for you. Even if you do encounter a bump along the road, expecting it is going to ruin hours, months, or even years of your life. Expect the best, have faith in yourself that if you are doing the right things, the right things will come your way. That way the bumps in the road will be dealt with in a positive and constructive manner, and you'll always have the future to look forward to.

"When it rains look for rainbows, when it's dark look for stars" - Oscar Wilde

Losses in life don't stick to your permanent record. If you've made a grave error or else been wronged in one way or another, don't focus on the negatives of that encounter. See some light in it. Because through having that bad experience, you have now learnt something about yourself, or the world, that you may not have known before. You have now been given the ability to look at things from a slightly different perspective. But don't take that opportunity to look at things from a pessimistic perspective, take that opportunity to become stronger as a result from it.

"God has given you this life because he knows you are strong enough to live it" - Unknown.

"Do not pray for an easy life, pray for the strength to endure a difficult one" - Bruce Lee

Challenges are not here to destroy us, they are here for our growth, believe it or not. How we react to certain obstacles and challenges that we are faced with will ultimately help build who we are, and expand our character for the better (if we allow it to). Have faith in yourself that you are someone that is here to grow, here to learn. Not somebody that's here to welcome the negative things in life into their reality. Every day we have a choice about how we react to every situation that comes into our path. Have you ever heard of the word "restriction"?

This to me sums up, in one word, how we should control our negative reactions, which only attract more pessimism into our lives anyway. Don't be fooled by the temporary fulfillment that negative emotions such as sadness and anger can give you. As in that moment it might feel like a natural or warranted reaction, but in the long run you have been drained of some of your power. If you can train your mind to not have that autopilot natural reaction to circumstances thrown at you, that is indeed one of the greatest powers you can possess. Understand that anything invalidating someone is projecting, they are most likely only doing as a result of an insecurity or a complex that they carry within themselves, and they are hurting themselves a lot more than they are hurting you.

"You've got to train your mind to be stronger than your emotions or else you'll lose to yourself every time" - Unknown

We hear a lot of bad news, lousy news, about CEO's doing the wrong thing, politicians lying and banks cheating. It would be very easy to let the news of the world dishearten us or anger us. If we trimmed the anger as a whole, most of the problems would fix themselves. Do not add to this storm of anger and negativity. If you look at the positive things over the negative, then you will attract more positivity into your life. Have faith that your positive outlook will attract positivity and vice versa. Don't find solace in being angry at something or someone, like so many others do. The same way certain music has different frequencies, and radio stations have different stations we tune into, it is scientifically tested that your thoughts vary to the same degree that different types of music does. If you're putting out negative, pessimistic thoughts, you might as well be playing those thoughts aloud and using your head as a speaker to do it. If you play that negative music around people and throughout the world everyday, then you're going to attract people, circumstances and scenarios that play that same music. Now imagine that you're playing a positive tune for the world to hear and give back to you! What a tremendously more enjoyable constructive and abundant life you would live! And here's the good news: you're in charge of your own radio station and you can flick to that channel whenever you want.

'Always pray to have eyes that see the best in people, a heart that forgives the worst, a mind that forgets the bad, and a soul that never loses faith'
- Unknown

Exercise:

Create a list of everything that excites you right now, and then a second list of all the things you are excited for, even if they seem unreachable. Read these two lists aloud 5 times daily. A tip to get into a really excitable, happy state, is to listen to your favourite songs whilst doing this exercise, as when you're listening to your favourite songs you will start to smile and feel uplifted. It is from here that you will naturally feel heightened in a state of positive emotions and therefore, when reading these things you are excited for, you will draw them into your reality much faster, through the feeling that they already exist. And that's the key. To feel them into existence.

Living over Existing

Everyone's got a right. Everyone's got a right to tell it how they see it. Everyone's got a right to entertain. Everyone's got a right to their own future. You might be born into a family where you are presumed by parents and the people around you to have a certain job, and live a certain life. To get married by a certain age, have kids by a certain age, make a certain amount of money due to a certain job at a certain age. But this is your life, not theirs. You've got a right to do what you want with your life. I'm aware some people live in incredibly controlled environments, some with incredibly wealthy parents and incredibly strict upbringings to poverty-stricken ones. From strict cultures that have been the way they are for centuries, to certain religions which shape your life in a very specific way. I understand that this might be hard for some of you to own and take responsibility for, but I do want you to always remember: your mind is your own. No one can take that away from you. The world is yours to design if you decide it is.

'A man can change his stars ' - A Knight's Tale, Movie.

Do you wake up and feel that you are moving forwards every day? Are you constantly in the same routine and never living in the moment? Get out of that hamster wheel you may be running on, like millions of others in this world, and start your new life today. Escape that mundane routine. There must be something that excites you. Follow that thing, ride that wave of excitement. We all have the same amount of time in the day, so if this new business endeavour is what excites you, then that should be your focus. The best thing you can do for yourself is to design a life you love, because then work will never feel like work, and you will look forward to every new day that's ahead. Carve your own destiny. Like a young child is constantly in a state of curiosity and excitement, that is how you should always be. Follow what excites you, and then you will attract more things that excite you and, ultimately, make you happy. I love to always be in a place of high excitement, as this is such a positive frequency to live in. Everyday, open your eyes to opportunities presenting themselves to you that will benefit you in your new abundant life you want to live, filled with the fruits of wealth and rich joyous moments. Never think that it's too late to do a 180 in your life; you are in control, and the moment you decide to live your life in a completely different manner, and commit to that manner, is the moment it will change. The world is your playground and your mind the child that's playing in it.

'Without dreams and goals there is no living, merely existing, and that is not why we are here.' - Mark Twain.

As wonderful as it is to have great ambitions, and even sometimes to reflect fondly on the past, remember that the present is all we really have. This is incredible news, and the way to utilise this news is to simply, as cliche as it sounds, live in the moment. Don't focus on something not working out, like a relationship, your hope for that promotion at work or passing an exam. Focus only on doing the best you can in the present to build towards those things working out. The power to be fully present is almost impossible to achieve, however, the more of you that is in the present, the more powerful your presence will be. Focusing on the past and the future takes some of your power and puts it in those respective places. Now those places don't really exist and so shouldn't be granted any of that power. In the scenarios that I mentioned earlier about exams etc., if you put all of your power into the present, i.e. enjoying that relationship you're in, working to the fullest of your capabilities, focusing on the exam when you are in the midst of it, you will give yourself the best possible shot at succeeding in all these areas and, just as important, you will enjoy the journey far, far more as it won't be filled with worry and anxiety.

Are you open to serendipity? Are you spontaneous? Are you open to life's surprises? Because I can tell you that some of the most magnificent things in my life have come from simply going with the strangest encounters when they were put in front of me. I cannot emphasise the quantity of incredible doors that having an openness to this will open for you too. In fact pretty much anything I have achieved has been a result of a surprise encounter that I just rolled with. As to what those encounters might be is totally unique for any individual, so I won't bother listing mine, but my point is that the best things happen unexpectedly. Are these unexpected circumstances, in fact, gifts from God's plan for each of us to receive, and appear as a code for us to unlock? I urge you to tap into the energy force of goodness that awaits you. I encourage you to see the potential light in every strange situation that comes before you, because as I said before, you never know where these things will lead you, but you know very well where not following them will: nowhere.

'The universe is always speaking to us, sending us little messages, causing coincidences and serendipities, reminding us to stop, to look around. To believe in something else, something more' - Nancy Thayer.

Exercise:

I'm going to give you a concept that might really resonate with you and might make a lot of the things we talked about clear, regarding living with clarity of mind. This exercise is commonly referred to as grounding. Basically what you are going to do is take off your shoes and walk around on the natural earth, as simple as that sounds. Think of it this way, the rubber on the soles of your shoes (providing that they're not made of wood) is directly prohibiting the energy resonating through the earth and passing through your body. Now even if you did somehow manage to get your hands on a pair of those cute Japanese sandals that are made of wood, you'd still be better off letting that energy pass directly through the soles of your feet. Often times in this modern world there's so much technology and a multitude of exterior sources really halting you from clear and grounded thought. Grounding was a huge part of my personal healing process when I was unwell,and I know it will help you too, regardless of the physical state of your body. Take a moment every day to gain some clarity on this world, ground yourself. You can do this in your own bedroom even, but better yet, go outside into nature, where natural untouched earth is present. Walk barefoot through these surroundings, see how it feels, let it affect you. Soak up that energy through our planet and let it flow through your whole being. Use it. Utilise it. Enjoy it.

"Man.

Because he sacrifices his health in order to make money.

Then he sacrifices money to recuperate his health.

And then he is so anxious about the future that he does not enjoy the present;

the result being that he does not live in the present or the future;

he lives as if he is never going to die, and then dies having never really lived."

– The 14th Dalai Lama

Gratitude over Complacency

Exercise:

Do you know the power that gratitude journaling has? It's one of my favourite morning ritual exercises to do, as it has such a feel-good factor to it. Try it now - write a list in your exercise journal of all the things you are grateful for today. It can even be something as small as your cup of tea. However big or small, add them all and surrender your gratitude that you have these things in your life. Start with the phrase "I am so grateful for..." or "I am thankful for...". Having gratitude will automatically attract more of those good things into your life as once you are in a place mentally of seeing the best in life, you will change your day, your month, even your year. Doing regular gratitude journaling will adjust the way you perceive situations because of your new-found positive focus.

When you focus on something greater than yourself, you will find that your problems will dissipate. By this, I mean that you will no longer have time to worry about what you lack and don't have, because you are distracted by helping someone that's got bigger problems than you do, or by doing a good deed, or through spreading some sort of love. It is in this place that you can re-evaluate your own situation and recognise how fortunate you actually are. If you only focus on yourself and on receiving for the self alone, you will eventually lose an objective view of this world. What an incredible thing it would be to leave a positive mark on this earth, and to leave everyone you have encountered feeling elevated after they had met you. When you give out this much positivity and love to others, you will feel positive and loved yourself, and there is no better state to be in for achieving than in a state where love is resonating through you.

"The more you express gratitude for what you have, the more likely you will have even more to express gratitude for" - Zig Ziglar

I am a firm believer in doing things for the right reasons. The reason and feeling behind something will not only impact whether or not it's achieved, but it will massively impact how you feel during and after said achievement. So regardless of your ambitions, never get complacent in thinking you don't have enough yet. Rather have the mindset that if you give out enough to others, and if you have enough faith in yourself and resonate gratitude in your words and actions, then your ambitions will come true. If you don't understand why something happened, then you will ultimately become complacent. Do not attribute your achievements to solely yourself and your gifts. Better yet, be grateful for your gifts and be grateful for the opportunities you've been given to showcase them, and I promise you that when you are, you will attract more of those opportunities as well as evolving your gifts. Maximise yourself - use your power in the right way for it to reach its full potential.

"Two things define you: Your patience when you have nothing and your attitude when you have everything." — George Bernard Shaw

If you practise gratitude in your day-to-day life, you will experience a better quality of life altogether. Taking moments in your day to recognise and reflect upon how wonderful it is to even be alive today is the best place to begin, and from there, look around and say thank you from your heart for all that you have. It's very easy to forget the things you already have and focus on the things you do not yet have. Your health is something you should always be grateful for, and it's even scientifically proven that having gratitude improves your immune system and sleep quality.

Be grateful for the people around you in particular. It costs nothing to be grateful for them. However, being ungrateful can cost you everything. Give any bit of credit where it's due. Not giving it to someone can leave a bad taste in people's mouths, but giving it will elevate them and you. Showing gratitude in front of people is a powerful thing. You will not only radiate gratefulness, you will also radiate modesty and humility. When you have achieved something, others will try to pull you down, especially if you show arrogance in these scenarios. There is no benefit to having arrogance or lack of humility. Make it impossible for them to pull you down, be untouchable and you will attract more like-minded people and more and more things to show gratitude for.

Now, once you start achieving greatness (or if you're already there now), you must first of all know how you got there. Understand what it was that got you there, appreciate it, appreciate the people who helped you along the way, because there is no such thing as a solely self-made successor. And you shouldn't want to be that. You should want to share the love and share the things to be grateful for. If you've got a spotlight on you, you make an unspoken agreement with the world to shine that spotlight on something for the greater good. This is receiving for the purpose of giving back. Give back to the world that gave something to you and receive great interest in return...

Tolerance Over Judgment

If you disagree or dislike something, that shouldn't in any way negatively affect you. It should be absolutely fine. Because if you felt bad every time you came across something you disliked or disagreed with you would feel bad quite often We are not in the business of feeling bad, we are in the business of feeling good, baby - all the time! The world will fix anything that needs to be fixed in time. Be tolerant, be patient. You will feel and be better off for it. Do not give power towards something you can't change; better again do not give power to something that there is no need to change.

"Compassion and tolerance are not a sign of weakness, but are a sign of strength" - Dalai Lama

Patience may feel hard to apply, particularly to anyone who presses your buttons, but those are the people you must show the most patience to, in fact. It is in these situations where you grow the most. You grow from the challenges, not from the good times. When you want to react the way you usually would to a situation you are confronted with unexpectedly, don't react. There is an opportunity ,for positive self-growth and change here - recognise it! Respond in the best possible way. So, if your initial reactions tend to steer towards anger or hurtful reactions,take a moment to breathe and ask yourself why this scenario could be showing up in your life? What are you meant to learn from it? After much practise of not being "reactive" to life's encounters you will feel so much happier and have a clearer outlook on life. Anger is a negative feeling, and mostly the person giving it out feels the worst from it. The other person will either laugh after and walk away feeling fine, or worse, you will have hurt someone through your unintentional angry words or tone. Be more tolerant and the world will seem like a much brighter place and, of course, give so much more back to you in return. We are here to evolve our nature from negative to positive. We need to change the robotic consciousness of receiving for the self alone to the desire to share with others. This will transform us into better people and help the world become a better place in turn.

"Everything that irritates us about others can lead us to an understanding of ourselves" - *Coral Young*

Understand yourself, and why exactly you would judge someone. Is it out of fear? Whatever it is, it's definitely not coming from a place of positivity and love. Most people have a fear of the unknown. Many years ago, when we were all from different tribes, so to speak, the act of fearing another tribe solely because they were foreign to you was quite ordinary. Something foreign often means unknown, the unknown leads to fear, fear leads to judgment. Judgment is a negative thing that should have no place in your heart, as you are solely hurting yourself and not the person you are judging. What an incredible world we would live in if everyone was tolerated and embraced for their differences! Be someone that spreads that incredible energy, and not the energy of judgment; don't give your power away so needlessly. If you do naturally find yourself judging someone, for whatever reason, figure out where it's coming from. Getting to the root of the problem is the easiest way to eliminate it. Once you realise it stems from something you don't want to feel you will find it a lot easier to not do it. Furthermore, learn about other people's faiths, cultures, or whatever it is you might be less tolerant towards. Understand why it is that they see the world the way they do, and that everyone's circumstances are completely different. Training yourself to see things from others perspectives is an incredible tool that will give you great empathy in life, and empathy leads to tolerance.

Exercise:

The benefits of Meditation are profound, and meditation has been scientifically proven to benefit our physical and mental health. Meditation is by far the best gift you can give yourself as often as you can. I like to do meditation as part of my morning ritual before I have really woken up fully, as my subconscious is still susceptible. This is a form of meditation sometimes known as mindfulness meditation. Firstly, sit or lay comfortably in a quiet place where you cannot be disturbed. Close your eyes and start breathing deeply for a few minutes, in through your nose and out through your mouth. Try to ensure that the exhales are double the length of the inhales. Focus on how your breath moves in through your nose until the final moment of your exhale, when it leaves through your mouth. If your attention drifts to something or someplace else, don't criticise yourself, just slowly bring it back to your breath. Set a timer and do this for around ten minutes to half an hour. This will calm your mind, open up neural pathways and overall leave you feeling so much better.

Love over Hate

"If I speak in the tongues of men and of angels, but have not love, I am only a resounding gong or a clanging cymbal. If I have the gift of prophecy and can fathom all mysteries and all knowledge, and if I have a faith that can move mountains, but have not love, I am nothing. If I give all I possess to the poor and surrender my body to the flames, but have not love, I gain nothing." - Corinthians 13.

Even if you possess all of the powerful mindset tools one may possess, such as astounding courage to never fear the unknown, massive faith in oneself, the giving of gratitude in multitudes; without love there is no real purpose to any of those things. Whatever you do, if you do not do it with love you will not feel love in return, and you will ultimately never be as happy as you deserve to be. Spread love, receive love. For, if everyone on this earth put love before anything else, the world would be a solely happy place. The reason you do anything is as important as the endeavour you are taking itself. Do things for the right reason and you will feel right in what you do. And remember this; anything bad that anyone bestows upon you, they are simply bestowing upon themselves twice over. Do not react in kind, rather send them love in return as there is no loss and only gain in doing so.

"Darkness cannot drive out darkness: only light can do that. Hate cannot drive out hate: only love can do that." - Martin Luther King Jr.

Self-love is a fundamental part of giving love, as if you don't love yourself you will have no love to give to anyone else. How often do you criticise yourself? Most people do it multiple times a day without even realising it. Understand that you are human, and not only is it absolutely fine to make mistakes, but it's a critical part on one's journey to understanding who they are. Give yourself compassion in a moment of error. Error is essential to growth and there is no losing, only learning. Love yourself for understanding that and wanting to learn. Seeing yourself as good enough is a powerful thing. When you have patience and compassion with yourself you will see the world in a more optimistic light and therefore, naturally giving more love and positivity to everyone you encounter, and by doing so, leaving them greatly elevated, and in turn yourself as well.

Inner child; Definition: "A person's supposed original or true self, when regarded as concealed in adulthood."- Oxford Dictionary.

Children are pure, innocent. Recognise that your inner child always exists (will always exist?), that your body is the temple for your soul and that your current mindset is easily corrupted by the negativity that the world can at times corrupt us with (if we allow it to). We are enforced in this modern world to neglect our inner child, suppress it. The seriousness of life and its everyday struggles pushes the inner child away for most people, which is sad. Nurture that inner child instead, as this is the best way to heal yourself from past hurt and pain. Disappointment can also be avoided through constant self-love and communicating with your inner self/child. Do not lose that wonderful excitement, awe and curiosity that you are naturally supposed to have - these are incredibly magnetic traits. Keep in tune with your inner child, ask him/her how they are genuinely feeling today and respond accordingly. Forgive yourself, say sorry to yourself and accept your apology. Tell yourself "I love you" as there are no more powerful words on this earth than that simple phrase.

Whenever in doubt about anything, remember this: You are not normal. You are a superior entity. You have already beat monumental odds - and you can do it again. Before you were even born you won a race over a million other potential lives. You are powerful. Harness your Courage, Certainty, Authenticity, Faith, Gratitude, Tolerance and, most importantly, Love. Harness your superpower - and beat the odds again. Make that decision today.

Exercises for you to practise

Ice Water:

How:

This is sometimes easier after you have already warmed through with a hot shower, however, this is not necessary. Simply go into your shower or bath and set it to the coldest setting, breathe deeply to help yourself endure the cold. Start with 5 seconds and build up to a few minutes a day. It will get easier and easier, and more and more beneficial.

Why:

- Improves your immune system
- Improves sleep quality
- Decreases stress
- Improves circulation, increasing your resistance to the cold
- Lowers depression levels by releasing more noradrenaline
- Improves fertility, hot baths can do the opposite
- Helps your muscles recover faster from a workout
- Enhances your skin and hair by reducing the lack of natural oils as well as strengthening the grip of the hair to the scalp

Wim Hof Breathing Exercise:

How:

"While sitting in a comfortable place, take 30 quick, deep breaths, inhaling through your nose and exhaling through your mouth. Then, take a deep breath and exhale; hold until you need to breathe in. Inhale again, as deep as you can, and hold it for 10 seconds. Repeat as many times as you like." - Discover Magazine.

Why:

- This will improve your mental clarity and focus, promoting loss of irrational anxiety
- Reduces stress, enabling you to live life to the fullest
- Better sleep quality, for a clearer conscience
- Enhances creativity, counteracting your fear of the unknown
- Improvement in sport's performance and recovery, making physical exercise easier and even more beneficial

Positive Affirmations:

How:

Write a list of positive affirmations that begin with "I AM…" followed by a positive word that describes who you are and who you want to be someday. Learn these by heart, and every morning, stand in your power with your feet firmly on the ground and smile as you read these aloud.

Why:

- The act of smiling releases endorphins and will put you in a more positive frame of mind
- It can instantly change your mood from negative to positive which attracts more good things to happen to you
- Has been shown to decrease health-deteriorating related stress
- Has been shown to help us dismiss harmful health threats
- Repetition of this will sink the affirmations into your subconscious, making you believe it and in turn making it a reality

List of Excitement:

How:

Create a list of everything that excites you right now, and then a second list of all the things you are excited for, even if they seem unreachable. Read this list aloud 5 times daily. A tip to get into a really excitable happy state is to listen to your favourite songs whilst doing this exercise, as when you're listening to your favourite songs you will start to smile and feel uplifted. It is from here that you will naturally feel heightened in a state of positive emotions.

Why:

- With constant focus on excitement you will attract more exciting things through really feeling that they are possible and as though they already exist
- Excitement makes you more likely to act upon your goals

- Increases a kind of hormone connected to your feelings, making them more powerful
- Triggers the endocrine system, increasing oxygen to the brain
- Encourages a form of playfulness into your life, attracting more exciting things

Grounding:

How:

Take off your shoes and walk around on the natural earth outside; connecting yourself with nature and the earth. Feel the energy from our planet soaking up through the soles of your feet, energising you.

Why:

- Neutralises free radicals as it pushes away electrical fields from the body
- Improves sleep quality and decreased inflammation, both as a result of normalising cortisol (the stress hormone)
- Improves pain management, shown to work for several different kinds of pain
- Improves immunity, helping the natural defences of the body to be restored

Gratitude Journaling:

How:

Write a list in your journal of all the things you are grateful for today, it can even be something as small as the cup of tea you're drinking right now! However big or small, add them all and feel thankful as you write them.Start with the phrase “I am so grateful for…” or “I am thankful for…”.

Why:

- It will instantly shift your day from negative to positive
- It will adjust the way you perceive situations because of your new-found positive focus.
- Improves self-esteem
- Improves mental strength, helping you overcome trauma
- Gratitude enhances your empathy for others and reduces your aggression towards them

Meditation:

How:

Firstly, sit or lay comfortably in a quiet place where you cannot be disturbed. Close your eyes and start breathing deeply for a few minutes, in through your nose and out through your mouth, try and ensure that the exhales are double the length of the inhales. Focus your breath on how it moves in through your nose and how it leaves, until the final moment of your exhale. If your attention drifts to something else, don’t criticise yourself, just slowly bring it back to your breath. Set a timer and do this for around ten minutes to half an hour.

Why:

- Clears your mind of unneeded subconscious clutter, giving you greater clarity

- Improves focus, preventing little distractions that are taking away from the important things in life
- Lessens impulsive reactions
- Shown to improve memory
- Shown to improve relationship satisfaction

Printed in Great Britain
by Amazon

72613498R00033